CHICAGO BEARS

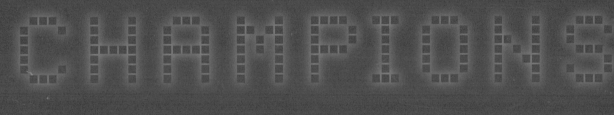

SUPER BOWL

Published by Creative Education
123 South Broad Street
Mankato, Minnesota 56001
Creative Education is an imprint of The Creative Company.

DESIGN AND PRODUCTION BY **EVANSDAY DESIGN**

LIBRARY OF CONGRESS CATALOGING-IN-PUBLICATION DATA

Frisch, Aaron.
Chicago Bears / by Aaron Frisch.
p. cm. — (Super Bowl champions)
Includes index.
ISBN 1-58341-381-2
1. Chicago Bears (Football team)—Juvenile literature. I. Title. II. Series.
GV956.C5F74 2005
796.332'64'0977311—dc22   2005048358

9 8 7 6 5 4 3 2

COVER PHOTO: quarterback Rex Grossman

PHOTOGRAPHS BY
AP/Wide World Photos, Corbis (Bettmann), Getty Images (Jonathan Daniel, Andy Lyons/ALLSPORT), Icon Sports Media Inc., SportsChrome USA

CHICAGO BEARS

The Bears have played many football games in the snow ^

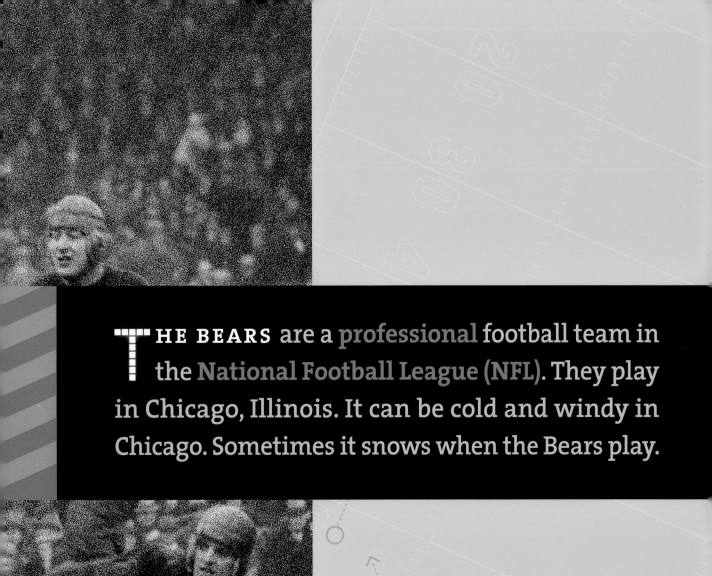

THE BEARS are a professional football team in the National Football League (NFL). They play in Chicago, Illinois. It can be cold and windy in Chicago. Sometimes it snows when the Bears play.

THE BEARS play in a stadium called Soldier Field. Their helmets are blue with an orange "C" on the side. Their uniforms are blue, orange, and white. The Bears play many games against teams called the Lions, Packers, and Vikings.

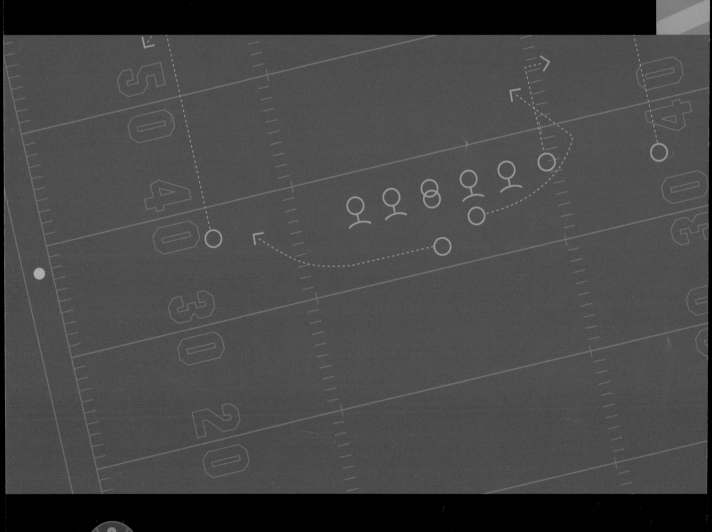

THE BEARS played their first season in 1921. Their first coach was named George Halas. He was the owner of the team for 64 years, too. Fans called him "Papa Bear."

Fast running back Gale Sayers scored lots of touchdowns ^

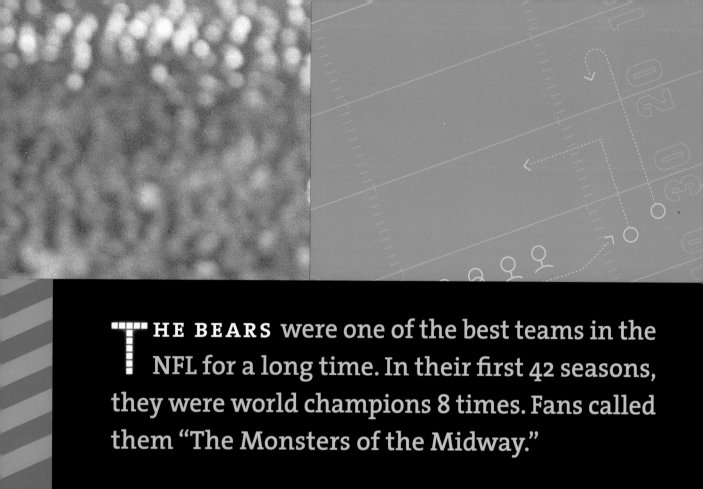

THE BEARS were one of the best teams in the NFL for a long time. In their first 42 seasons, they were world champions 8 times. Fans called them "The Monsters of the Midway."

IN 1940, the Bears beat the Washington Redskins 73–0 to become champions. It was the most lopsided game ever in the NFL.

Chicago's uniforms and helmets were simpler in 1940 ^

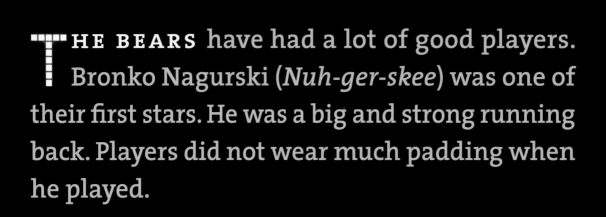

THE BEARS have had a lot of good players. Bronko Nagurski (*Nuh-ger-skee*) was one of their first stars. He was a big and strong running back. Players did not wear much padding when he played.

Bronko Nagurski (right) was a strong runner and blocker

DICK BUTKUS was a linebacker. He tackled so hard that a lot of players on other teams were afraid of him! Walter Payton was a running back. He played 13 seasons. He set a record by running with the ball for more yards than any NFL player had before.

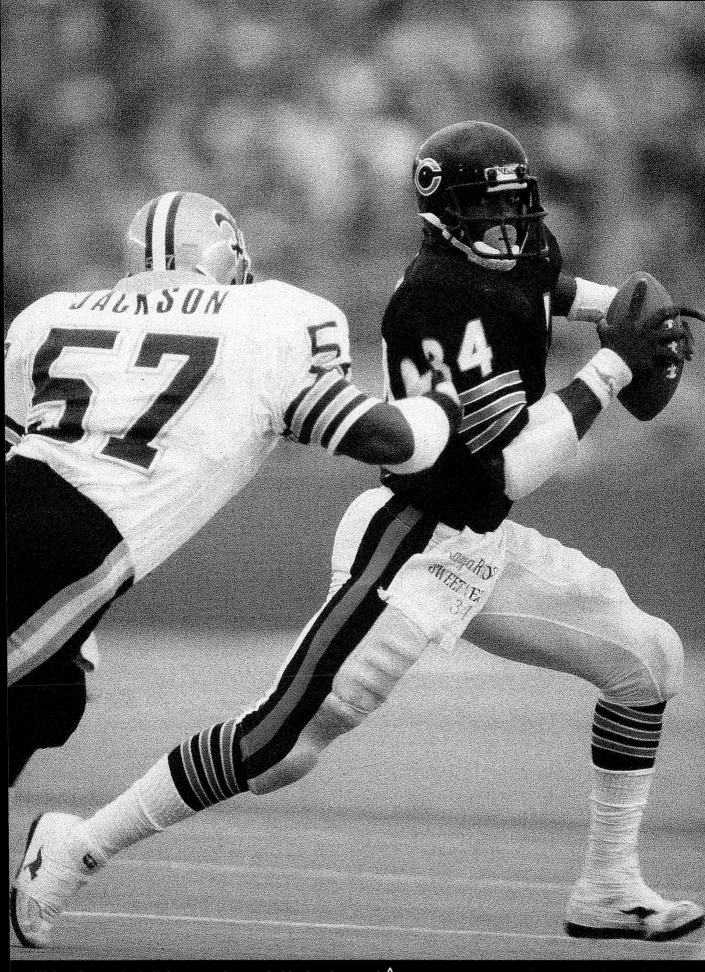

Walter Payton had slick moves that made him hard to catch ^

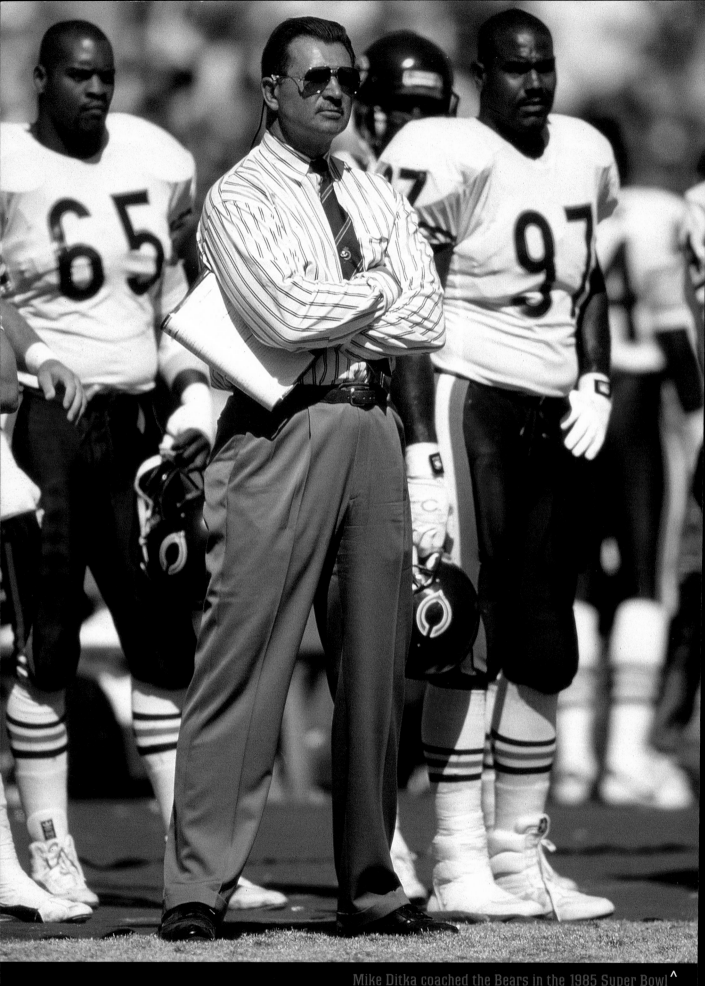

Mike Ditka coached the Bears in the 1985 Super Bowl ^

IN 1985, the Bears won 15 games and lost only 1. Then they beat the New England Patriots 46–10 in the Super Bowl. It was one of the easiest Super Bowl wins ever. It made the Bears world champions again.

ONE OF the Bears' best players today is Brian Urlacher (*Er-lak-er*). He is a big and fast linebacker. Bears fans hope that he will help the team win the Super Bowl again!

Brian Urlacher tackled hard and was a team leader ^

lopsided
uneven, like when one team wins a game very easily

National Football League (NFL)
a group of football teams that play against each other;
there are 32 teams in the NFL today

professional
a person or team that gets paid to play or work

record
something that is the best (or most) ever

Team colors
Blue, orange, and white

Home stadium
Soldier Field (61,500 seats)

Conference/Division
National Football Conference (NFC), North Division

First season
1921

Super Bowl win
1985 (beat New England Patriots 46–10)

Training camp location
Bourbonnais, Illinois

Bears Web site for kids
http://www.chicagobears.com/fancenter/kids.jsp

NFL Web site for kids
http://www.playfootball.com/

INDEX